My Reason for writing this book.

I am confident that you will find the content of this book to be incredibly helpful, supportive, and engaging. Before I dive into the details, I want to emphasize that there is no judgment on my part, and this book is not a plea to seek out a mentor or business coach. Rather, it is a reflection of my own experiences and a recognition that in today's fast-paced world of technology and innovation, those of us who have taken the brave step of venturing into business on our own may eventually require assistance.

Through real-life examples, I aim to empower you to form your own opinions on this important topic. In this book, I will strive to captivate you with valuable and accurate information, highlighting the benefits of partnering with a mentor or coach in building a successful business, as opposed to going it alone.

With my extensive experience and unique perspective, I can bring significant value to your endeavours. Please don't hesitate to ask any questions or explore potential business strategies together. My ultimate goal is to see your business soar to new heights.

I bring a proven track record of unparalleled success in civil engineering and business development, spearheading major projects across Europe, the UK, and NZ for esteemed organisations. As a visionary entrepreneur, I have established and successfully sold multiple businesses, provided guidance to CEOs, and authored publications on entrepreneurship. My unwavering passion lies in nurturing and empowering small and medium-sized enterprises to achieve remarkable growth and prosperity.

Having been married three times, I have accumulated invaluable personal wisdom that has profoundly influenced my outlook on life. Enduring financial highs and lows has underscored the significance of making astute financial decisions and appreciating money in a prudent manner. Although far from flawless, I place a premium on humility, integrity, and transparency in every facet of my existence. My overarching aspiration is to inspire and assist others in attaining triumph in their personal and professional endeavors, steering them towards establishing prosperity and enterprises that align with their core beliefs.

Title: The Pitfalls of Going Solo: Why You Should Consider Collaborating for Business Success

]\

Embarking on the journey of starting a business may seem like a dream come true, with the promise of independence and control. However, the reality of entrepreneurship can be overwhelming, especially if you choose to go it alone. While the idea of being a sole proprietor may be enticing, there are compelling reasons why collaboration and partnership are essential for long-term success.

Asking for help in business can be a strategic decision that leads to growth, innovation, and success.
Here are several reasons why seeking assistance can be beneficial: Expertise and Knowledge: Collaborating with others can bring in specialized skills and knowledge that you may lack. This can lead to better decision-making and innovative solutions. Networking Opportunities; Asking for help can expand your professional network.

Connecting with others can lead to partnerships, mentorships, and potential customers.

Different Perspectives:

Engaging with others can provide new viewpoints that challenge your assumptions and lead to improved strategies and ideas.

Time Efficiency: Delegating tasks or seeking assistance can free up your time to focus on core business activities and strategic planning, enhancing overall productivity.

Problem-Solving: Collaborating with others can help identify and solve problems more effectively. A diverse team can bring various solutions to the table.

Accountability: Seeking help can create a support system that keeps you accountable.

Partners, mentors, or advisors can provide motivation and guidance to achieve your goals.

Resource Access: Others may have access to resources, tools, or funding that can help your business grow. By contacting you, you may find opportunities that were previously unavailable to you. Building a Supportive Community: Asking for help fosters relationships and creates a community that can provide support during challenging times, which is especially valuable in the often-isolated world of entrepreneurship.

Learning and Development: Engaging with others allows for continuous learning. You can gain insights from their experiences and mistakes, which can inform your own business practices. Improved Morale and Well-Being: Running a business can be stressful. Seeking help can lighten the load and improve your mental well-being, allowing you to approach challenges more clearly.

In summary, asking for help in business is not a sign of weakness; instead, it is a strategic approach that can lead to personal and professional growth, better decision-making, and increased opportunities for success

Isolation and Limited Networking Opportunities: Managing a business alone can be isolating, with few chances to network and establish connections with fellow entrepreneurs and industry experts. Cultivating a strong network is crucial for business triumph, as it can result in valuable partnerships, collaborations, and mentorship opportunities.

Working with others can help expand your network and open doors to new opportunities.

Embrace Accountability: Engaging partners or a board of advisors in your decision-making process is crucial for gaining diverse perspectives and making well-informed, strategic choices for your business. Avoid the pitfall of solitary decision-making - embrace accountability to drive your business towards success.

Avoid Burnout and Overwhelm: In the fast-paced world of entrepreneurship, the pressure can be intense and the demands never-ending. To succeed, you must possess unwavering determination, exceptional decision-making abilities, and the capacity to handle numerous tasks simultaneously. When you go it alone in business, the risk of burnout and overwhelm skyrockets as you bear the weight of all responsibilities without any backup. By assembling a team of committed employees or partners, not only will you lighten your load, but you'll also receive crucial support during challenging periods.

In conclusion, it is undeniable that embarking on the entrepreneurial journey solo may seem enticing. However, the harsh reality is that the risks and obstacles of going it alone in the business realm are immense. By joining forces, forging partnerships, and embracing teamwork, you open the door to a treasure trove of expertise, resources, networking opportunities, and support that will significantly amplify your chances of achieving long-term success. Always remember that constructing a thriving business necessitates the combined effort of a community, and going solo on this path may not be the most effective route to take.

The Pitfalls of Going Solo: Why You Should Not Do Business on Your Own

Starting a business can be an exhilarating journey, filled with the promise of being your own boss and making all the decisions. However, the road to entrepreneurship can be overwhelming, especially when you're going it alone. While the idea of running a business solo may seem attractive, there are numerous reasons why there may be better choices., we will delve into the pitfalls of doing business independently and why collaboration and partnership could be the key to achieving long-term success.

Lack of Expertise:

Running your business solo can be incredibly challenging due to the lack of expertise in various areas. You need skills in marketing, finance, operations, human resources, and more to ensure your business thrives. Instead of struggling alone, why not consider the benefits of collaborating with experts who bring different skills to the table? By working together and combining your strengths, you can build a more successful and sustainable business in the long run.

Maximise Your Resources: Launching and expanding a business requires a significant investment of resources—funds, time, and effort. Going it alone can severely limit your growth potential and hinder your ability to stand out in a competitive market. By partnering with investors or collaborators, you can unlock access to invaluable resources that can accelerate your business's expansion.

Break the Isolation Barrier: Running a business on your own can be isolating, leaving you with limited opportunities to network and connect with fellow entrepreneurs and industry experts. Embrace the power of collaboration to enhance your journey, gain fresh insights, and build a supportive network that propels your success.

Creating a robust network is absolutely crucial for achieving business success, as it opens doors to invaluable partnerships, collaborations, and mentorship opportunities.

Working with others can help expand your network and open doors to new opportunities.

Lack of Accountability: As the sole decision-maker in your business, it's crucial to avoid falling into the trap of making decisions in isolation. Seeking feedback and considering different perspectives is essential for making informed and strategic decisions. By having partners or a board of advisors, you can ensure greater accountability and drive success for your business.

Burnout and Overwhelm: Entrepreneurship is undoubtedly a challenging journey, filled with long hours, constant decision-making, and the pressure of wearing multiple hats. Going it alone can quickly lead to burnout and overwhelm as you try to manage all aspects of the business single-handedly. Building a team of employees or partners can help alleviate the workload and provide invaluable support during tough times.

In conclusion, recognising the immense advantages of collaboration in entrepreneurship is vital. Joining forces with others brings invaluable expertise, resources, networking opportunities, and support essential for achieving long-term success. Building a thriving business is a team endeavour, and choosing to go it alone may significantly limit your potential. Embrace collaboration and unlock the full spectrum of opportunities that can propel your business forward.

Embarking on a business venture is an exhilarating opportunity that empowers you to take charge and make impactful decisions that shape your success.

Embarking on the journey of entrepreneurship can definitely be challenging, particularly when navigating it solo. While the thought of managing a business independently may be attractive, there are numerous compelling reasons why collaborating with others could lead to greater success.

Starting a business is undeniably thrilling, with the promise of independence and full control over your destiny. However, the path of entrepreneurship can be overwhelming, particularly when navigating it solo. Although the idea of being a lone wolf in the business world may be tempting, there are compelling reasons why seeking collaboration and partnerships could be pivotal in achieving sustained success. In this blog, we will delve into the drawbacks of going alone and highlight the benefits of working together for long-term prosperity.

A business venture is an opportunity that is enticed with the promise of autonomy and control. Yet, navigating the entrepreneurial landscape solo can be overwhelming. Despite the initial appeal of running a business independently, it's crucial to acknowledge the potential drawbacks. In this book, we will delve into the disadvantages of going alone and illustrate how collaboration and partnerships can pave the way for sustained success.

We will delve into the dangers of going solo in business and emphasize why joining forces through collaboration and partnerships can pave the way for lasting success.

Expertise Deficit:

Trying to navigate the complexities of entrepreneurship alone can be daunting, especially when faced with the myriad of skills needed for success. From marketing and finance to operations and human resources, a thriving business demands a diverse range of expertise. Without a team of specialists at your side, it's easy to feel

overwhelmed and struggle to effectively manage all facets of your venture.

Maximise Your Potential:
Building and expanding a business typically requires substantial resources such as funds, effort, and commitment. Going solo might require more essential resources to elevate your business and thrive in a competitive market.

Collaborating with partners or investors can provide access to additional resources and help fuel the growth of your business.

Unlock the Power of Networking: Don't let isolation hold back your business success. By connecting with fellow entrepreneurs and industry experts, you can unlock valuable partnerships, collaborations, and mentorship opportunities that can take your business to new heights. Expand your network and watch as new doors open to endless possibilities.

Lack of Accountability: Being the sole decision-maker in your business may lead to overlooking important perspectives and missing out on valuable feedback. By having partners or a board of advisors, you can establish accountability and make well-informed, strategic decisions for the success of your business.

Managing burnout and overwhelm is crucial in the world of entrepreneurship. With the constant demands and pressures of running a business solo, it's easy to feel drained and overwhelmed. By building a strong team of employees or partners, you can alleviate the load, share responsibilities, and have the support you need to thrive during tough times. Don't let burnout hinder your success - surround yourself with a reliable team and watch your business flourish.

In conclusion, it is crucial to recognize the undeniable benefits of collaboration, partnership, and teamwork in the world of entrepreneurship. By joining forces with others, you can tap into a wealth of expertise, resources, networking opportunities, and support that can dramatically enhance your chances of achieving long-term success.

Keep in mind, collaborating with others is crucial for building a thriving business, and trying to do it all alone may not lead to the best results.

While it is possible to run a successful business on your own, working with others can provide valuable expertise, resources, and support that can help increase your chances of success in the long run and save you time whilst building your business effectively.

Table of Contents:

1. The Power of Connection: Building Relationships for Success

2. Overcoming Obstacles: Strategies for Strength and Resilience

3. Seeking Support: The Strength in Asking for Help

4. The Importance of Collaboration: Achieving More Together

5. Finding Your Tribe: Establishing a Support System for Growth

6. Embracing Vulnerability: Authenticity in Relationships

7. The Value of Mentorship: Learning from Others for Progress

8. Building Resilience: Bouncing Back from Challenges

9. Navigating Change: Adapting and Thriving in a Dynamic World

Let's Celebrate Success: Recognizing Achievements and Spreading Joy!

Unleash the Power of Connection: Transform Relationships into Pathways to Success and Triumph over Challenges. Arm Yourself with Strategies to Conquer Obstacles and Emerge Stronger than Ever. Don't Hesitate to Seek Support: It's a Sign of Strength, not Weakness. Harness the Strength of Collaboration for Unprecedented Achievements. Build Your

Dream Team: Establish a Support Network that Empowers You to Flourish. Embrace Your Vulnerability and Witness the Birth of Authentic Connections. Embrace Mentorship to Propel Yourself to New Heights. Develop Resilience: Master the Art of Bouncing Back from Adversity. Navigate Change with Grace and Thrive in a World of Constant Evolution. Celebrate Your Victories and Share Your Triumphs with the World.

Chapter 1: The Power of Connection

In today's fast-paced and cutthroat business world, the power of making meaningful connections cannot be underestimated. The ability to foster strong relationships with clients, colleagues, and industry peers is not just important, it's essential for the growth and success of your business. By networking effectively at industry events, conferences, and other gatherings, you have the chance to expand your circle, share insights, and forge connections that can potentially lead to lucrative business ventures. Networking isn't just about socializing - it's about staying ahead of the curve, being in the know about industry trends, and seizing opportunities for collaboration and growth. And let's not forget the importance of nurturing existing client relationships; maintaining these connections is the lifeblood of your business. So, don't underestimate the power of networking and relationship-building in achieving your business goals.

By consistently providing exceptional customer service, fulfilling all commitments, and exceeding client expectations, you can establish a devoted customer following and ensure continued business from repeat customers.

Establishing trust and credibility with clients is crucial for achieving long-term success in the business world. Collaboration is a vital component in building strong connections in business. By forging partnerships with other businesses, suppliers, and industry peers, you can gain access to valuable resources, knowledge, and opportunities that may be otherwise out of reach.

Building connections is absolutely crucial for achieving success in any industry. While networking events are a good starting point, the real key to growth and success lies in cultivating authentic relationships. In my upcoming book, I will share my personal journey and insights to underscore the transformative impact of having a mentor. If you are truly committed to excelling in your field, having a mentor is not just important - it's a game-changer. To truly position yourself as an authority and differentiate yourself from the competition, it is essential to carefully strategize how you market and sell your business. Allow me to guide you on the path to success.

I have an incredibly powerful and inspiring true story that I can't wait to share with you. It's about a business that came to me for guidance because they were determined to take their operations to the next level. With two thriving locations and a dedicated team of 23 employees, the owner knew that they were capable of so much more. Despite having good sales, they were struggling to meet the quality and quantity targets they had set at the beginning of the year.

When I asked about their strategy to reach these goals, the owner revealed a detailed plan that he had kept to himself. He believed that by keeping full control, he could steer the business in the right direction. Little did he know, there was a better way. Let me share with you how we worked together to revolutionize his approach and achieve incredible results.

I delved deeper into the reasoning behind his decision to withhold his plan. He eloquently explained the competitive advantage it provides, allowing him to selectively choose top performers to pave the way for others to follow. I emphasized the critical importance of achieving his goals and objectives. He reiterated the vital role they play in driving growth and financial prosperity. Finally, I discussed the pivotal role his team plays in executing his strategy, underscoring their indispensable contribution.

After further discussions, I delved into the areas where he identified weaknesses in his plan. He acknowledged that the figures were falling short of his weekly targets and his team's motivation levels were not improving. I inquired about why his groundbreaking vision was not producing the desired outcomes in elevating his team's performance.

Now, let me provide some feedback and assistance. I can tell you've probably already come up with your own ideas on why this plan isn't working for my client.

My analysis is broken down into three crucial parts. Firstly, in order to truly engage his team and align everyone towards a common goal, it is imperative for him to openly communicate his plan and vision. Secondly, by singling out top performers and unfairly burdening them with higher expectations, he runs the risk of breeding discord and animosity within the team. To cultivate a harmonious and efficient work environment, it is paramount for him to involve all team members and treat them equitably. I am confident you will concur.

Secondly, I asked how he came up with the conclusion to leave his people out of his plan and how he thought he could motivate them every day to achieve and perform better given that he was the only one privy to the plan.

And finally, I had to firmly urge him to develop a new strategy that involved effectively communicating his vision to his team and breaking it down into manageable tasks for better oversight and measurement of outcomes. It is crucial that he considers a collaborative approach to enhance his effectiveness and clarity on his vision. Instead of excluding his team members, he must embrace inclusivity to foster a positive impact on both himself and his team. Moving forward, success lies in uniting his team and fostering a culture of teamwork. I emphasized the importance of all team members working together harmoniously, rather than solely relying on individual top performers.

Crucial step in the operation was to gather his team and seek their input on their perception of the business vision before

outlining his plan. Through this process, we uncovered key insights that highlighted the necessity for this talented leader to acquire new skills he had previously overlooked. It was eye-opening for him to realise that his team had little understanding of his goals and challenges and were under the impression that they were already meeting his targets for the business.

With humility, he acknowledged that the missing link in his plan was his team, and their lack of cohesion needed to be improved in the achievement of his goals.

This exceptional leader has surpassed all expectations and achieved incredible success beyond his wildest dreams. Our close friendship has flourished over the years as we continue to work together. To highlight his remarkable accomplishments, he now oversees a workforce of more than one hundred and fifty employees.

The crucial message to grasp is that mistakes are a part of everyone's journey, and believe me, I've had my fair share in the past. Having a supportive partner to guide you and refine your strategies is essential for creating a lasting impact. Going solo can hinder your advancement and hinder your achievements.

Chapter 2: Conquering Obstacles: Empowering Strategies for Strength and Resilience

In the journey of life and business, obstacles are inevitable. They serve as tests of our strength and resilience, but also as opportunities for growth and learning. This chapter will reveal powerful strategies for overcoming obstacles and building the strength and resilience needed to conquer adversity. The first crucial step in overcoming obstacles is to confront them directly. Avoiding or ignoring challenges will only prolong the inevitable and potentially lead to even greater hardships. By confronting obstacles head-on and acknowledging the reality of the situation, you can start devising a plan to conquer them.

Maintaining a positive mindset is also essential in overcoming obstacles. While challenges may seem overwhelming, a positive attitude can help you remain focused, driven, and resilient in adversity. You can approach obstacles with optimism and determination by viewing them as opportunities for personal growth and development. Seeking support from others is crucial when facing obstacles. Whether seeking advice from a mentor, relying on loved ones for emotional support, or collaborating with colleagues to find solutions, reaching out to others can provide valuable insights, guidance, and encouragement during tough times.

Embracing adaptability and flexibility in facing obstacles is crucial for conquering challenges. By being willing to modify your strategies, experiment with new methods, and make necessary changes, you can effectively overcome obstacles and uncover innovative solutions. Success in overcoming challenges requires strength and resilience and a proactive approach in tackling hurdles with determination.

Take control of your future by harnessing these powerful strategies and seizing the opportunity to grow and thrive in the face of challenges. Transform into a stronger, more resilient individual poised to conquer any obstacles that cross your path. Don't let this chance to elevate your skills and effortlessly navigate life and business slip away. If you're serious about overcoming your obstacles, reach out to me now and let's embark on a journey of transformation through our unparalleled training and coaching programs.

Chapter 3: Seeking Support: The Strength in Asking for Help

In a society that frequently emphasizes the importance of independence and self-reliance, it is common to view asking for help as a weakness. Yet, it is vital to recognize that seeking support is not only a sign of strength, but also a crucial skill that can pave the way for personal development, resilience, and achievement.

In this chapter, we will explore the essential role of seeking support and the empowerment that comes from reaching out for assistance. Contrary to common misconceptions, asking for help does not indicate weakness. Instead, it demonstrates bravery and openness. It requires great strength to recognize when you need guidance or cannot manage everything on your own.

By embracing the courage to seek assistance, you showcase a commendable level of humility and a strong desire for personal development. Opening yourself up to support not only allows you to expand your understanding but also grants you access to invaluable perspectives and insights. Utilising the expertise and knowledge of others through seeking help is a powerful tool for your own growth and success.

Unlock the transformative power of seeking advice and guidance from mentors, colleagues, and friends. By tapping into their invaluable insights, you can conquer challenges, make informed decisions, and achieve your goals with confidence. Embracing support not only enhances your emotional and psychological well-being, but it also lays a solid foundation for your success. Don't underestimate the unparalleled advantages that come from reaching out—this simple act can propel you toward extraordinary outcomes.

Sharing your struggles and challenges with others can help you feel less alone and more supported. When you allow yourself to be vulnerable and open up to others, you create opportunities for connection, empathy, and understanding that can help

<u>you cope with difficult situations and build resilience.</u>

Embracing support is essential for fostering collaboration and teamwork. When you seek assistance from others, you open doors to collaborative efforts, creative brainstorming sessions, and effective problem-solving strategies. Joining forces with others can result in groundbreaking solutions, collective achievements, and deeper connections founded on trust and mutual assistance.

In conclusion, seeking support is not a sign of weakness, but a demonstration of strength and courage. By asking for help, you open yourself up to new perspectives, insights, and opportunities for growth. Embracing the strength in seeking support can help you navigate challenges, build resilience, and achieve greater success in both your personal and professional life.

Chapter 4: The Importance of Collaboration: Achieving More Together

In today's interconnected world, collaboration is not just helpful, but

absolutely crucial for achieving success in both personal and professional pursuits. By joining forces with others, individuals can unlock their full potential and accomplish far more than they ever could alone. Together, we can harness our combined strengths, knowledge, and assets to achieve our shared goals. In the following chapter, we will delve into the profound impact of collaboration and the multitude of advantages that come from working together towards common objectives.

Collaboration is the key to unlocking limitless creativity and groundbreaking innovation. By uniting individuals with unique backgrounds, experiences, and expertise, the possibilities for generating fresh ideas, inventive solutions, and cutting-edge approaches are endless. Through fostering a culture of open communication and collaboration, teams can ignite creativity and propel innovation to new heights in their endeavors.

Collaboration is essential for fostering continuous learning and skill enhancement. When individuals collaborate with others who bring diverse strengths and expertise to the table, they have the opportunity to absorb new knowledge, refine their skills, and acquire fresh abilities. This exchange of ideas and best practices among team members not only accelerates personal and professional growth but also creates a supportive environment for mentorship and mutual development.

Collaboration is absolutely essential for boosting efficiency and productivity in any team. When team members come together to work on a common project or goal, they can make the most of each other's strengths, assign tasks based on expertise, and streamline processes to achieve results faster and more effectively. By pooling resources and expertise, teams can easily overcome obstacles and tackle challenges head-on. Embracing collaboration is the key to success for any team.

Furthermore, collaboration is the key to building unbreakable bonds and cultivating a deep sense of belonging within a community. When individuals unite in pursuit of a shared objective, they cultivate a foundation of trust, admiration, and camaraderie among their fellow team members. Collaboration fuels teamwork, effective communication, and unwavering support, nurturing a work environment that is not only positive but also inclusive, where every individual is esteemed and empowered. In essence, the significance of collaboration lies in its ability to achieve far more collectively than individually.

By nurturing innovation, fostering continuous learning, bolstering efficiency, and forging strong connections, collaboration paves the way for unparalleled success, groundbreaking innovation, and unparalleled fulfillment in both personal and professional endeavors. Embracing the potential of collaboration empowers individuals and teams to soar to new heights and make a lasting impact in their communities and beyond.

Chapter 5: Finding Your Tribe: Establishing a Support System for Growth

Chapter 7: The Value of Mentorship: Learning from Others for Progress Mentorship

In life and in business, a strong support system is crucial for personal growth, resilience, and success. Your 'tribe' is made up of individuals who truly understand and uplift you, who align with your values and aspirations, and who push you to reach your full potential. Join us in this chapter as we delve into the significance of discovering your tribe and creating a support network that fosters your continuous growth and evolution.

Embrace the power of your tribe - a community that offers belonging, understanding, and unwavering support. Surround yourself with those who uplift you in times of triumph and stand by you in moments of challenge. Together, you will cultivate a network of like-minded individuals who share your vision and propel you towards personal and professional success.

Your tribe not only offers encouragement and motivation, but they are the driving force behind your success. They are the ones who wholeheartedly believe in you, who fearlessly push you to step out of your comfort zone, and who relentlessly challenge you to reach new heights. Your tribe serves as an unwavering source of inspiration and motivation, empowering you to stay laser-focused and unwaveringly committed to your goals, even in the face of daunting obstacles and setbacks. Joining forces with your tribe is the key to unlocking your full potential and achieving greatness.

Your tribe plays a crucial role in offering unwavering support and invaluable guidance. They are your go-to source for wise advice, constructive feedback, and fresh perspectives whenever you find yourself at a crossroads. Count on your tribe to lend a compassionate ear, a supportive shoulder, and a helpful hand during times of confusion or stress. Embracing the support and guidance of your tribe will equip you with the clarity, solutions, and motivation needed to conquer obstacles and make empowered choices.

Joining your tribe is the key to unlocking endless opportunities for collaboration and personal growth. Surround yourself with individuals who will push you to innovate, generously share their wisdom, and work together towards achieving common objectives.

By working together with your tribe, you can leverage each other's strengths, skills, and resources to achieve greater success and make a positive impact in your personal and professional endeavors. In conclusion, finding your tribe is essential for establishing a support system that nurtures your growth and development. By surrounding yourself with like-minded individuals who understand and support you, who provide encouragement and motivation, who offer support and guidance, and who foster collaboration and growth, you can create a community of allies and advocates who help you thrive and succeed. Embracing the power of finding your tribe can lead to personal fulfillment, professional success, and a sense of belonging and connection that enriches your life and work.

Chapter 6: Embracing Vulnerability:

Authenticity in Relationships: In a world that often values strength and perfection, embracing vulnerability is a powerful tool for cultivating authentic and meaningful relationships.

Vulnerability

is the key to showing your true self, being open and honest about your thoughts, feelings, and experiences, even when it may feel daunting.

This chapter will delve into the significance of embracing vulnerability in relationships and how it can pave the way for deeper connections, trust, and authenticity. Vulnerability nurtures genuine connections. When you allow yourself to be vulnerable, you create opportunities for more profound and meaningful relationships. By sharing your fears, insecurities, and struggles, you encourage others to do the same, fostering a foundation of trust, empathy, and understanding that strengthens your bond. Vulnerability fosters trust and authenticity. By being willing to be vulnerable and reveal your authentic self, you exhibit transparency and honesty in your relationships. Through open and honest communication about your thoughts, feelings, and experiences, you build trust and establish a safe environment for emotional intimacy and open dialogue. Vulnerability encourages empathy and compassion.

Opening up about your vulnerabilities allows others to empathize with your challenges and hardships.

By sharing your vulnerabilities, you create opportunities for others to demonstrate compassion, understanding, and support,

ultimately leading to deeper connections and a sense of shared humanity.

Vulnerability encourages growth and resilience. When you embrace vulnerability and allow yourself to be seen as you truly are, you create opportunities for personal growth and self-discovery.

Building resilience, courage, and self-acceptance starts with confronting your fears, insecurities, and vulnerabilities head-on. This powerful journey not only enhances your confidence but also fosters authenticity in your relationships and interactions. Embracing vulnerability is not just important; it is essential for cultivating authentic and meaningful connections. By revealing your true self and being open and honest about your thoughts and feelings, you invite deeper connections, trust, and empathy from others. When you allow yourself to be seen and accepted for who you truly are, you unlock incredible opportunities for growth and resilience. Embracing vulnerability enriches your life and nurtures a profound sense of connection and belonging—an essential foundation for your personal and emotional well-being.

Mentorship is an indispensable tool for unparalleled personal and professional growth. A mentor possesses the invaluable knowledge, experience, and wisdom to guide and empower you towards realising your dreams and ambitions.

This chapter delves into the pivotal role of mentorship and how absorbing insights from others can propel you towards unparalleled success. Mentorship serves as a beacon of guidance and support.

 A mentor can impart invaluable insights, advice, and perspectives based on their own rich experiences and expertise.

By seeking mentorship, you can harness

their wisdom, knowledge, and guidance to navigate challenges, make informed decisions, and achieve your goals with unwavering confidence and clarity. Mentorship nurtures personal and professional development.

A mentor can help you recognise your strengths, weaknesses, and areas for improvement, offering constructive feedback, encouragement, and unwavering support to help you unleash your full potential.

By learning from someone who has been where you want to go, you can gain valuable skills, knowledge, and strategies that can help you advance in your career and personal life. Mentorship promotes accountability and motivation. A mentor can help you set goals, create action plans, and track your progress towards achieving your objectives.

By holding you accountable and providing consistent encouragement and unwavering support, a mentor can empower you to remain resolute, enthusiastic, and dedicated to achieving your goals, regardless of obstacles and difficulties.

Mentorship not only cultivates networks but also fosters invaluable connections.

A mentor is the key to unlocking endless opportunities, connecting you with valuable resources and influential contacts to propel you towards unparalleled success in both your personal and professional endeavors.

Unlock endless possibilities for growth and success by tapping into your mentor's vast network and knowledge. With their guidance, you can unlock doors to new opportunities, forge powerful partnerships, and embark on collaborations that will drive you towards your goals.

Mentorship is a priceless asset that offers invaluable insights, guidance, and a direct path to success. Surround yourself with mentors who will not only empower, guide, and motivate you but also provide the much-needed support and direction to reach your full potential. Through their support, you can fast-track your personal and professional development, confidently achieve your aspirations, and cultivate meaningful connections that will enhance your journey.

Embrace the power of mentorship and watch as your life transforms with accelerated learning, unprecedented growth, and unparalleled success in every aspect.

Chapter 8: Building Resilience:

Mastering the Art of Bouncing Back: Resilience is not just about bouncing back from setbacks, it's about thriving in the face of adversity. It's about building the strength and determination to overcome obstacles and adapt to change gracefully and resiliently.

This chapter will explore powerful strategies for cultivating resilience, developing the right mindset, and returning from challenges more vital than ever.

Embrace adversity as a catalyst for growth and learning.

By confronting challenges directly, you can cultivate the resilience necessary to overcome any obstacle. It's all about maintaining a positive mindset. Focus on solutions, not problems, and view setbacks as opportunities to grow and learn. By adopting this mindset, you can bounce back from challenges with newfound strength and resilience, feeling more in control of your life.

Self-care is not just important, it's non-negotiable. Take care of yourself physically, emotionally, and mentally to build the resilience to navigate challenging times.

By practising self-care activities like exercise, mindfulness, and stress management, you can recharge and rejuvenate, ready to face any challenge that comes your way. And remember, you don't have to go it alone.

By prioritizing your self-care, you are valuing and prioritizing yourself.

Seek support from friends, family, colleagues, or mentors to gain valuable perspective, guidance, and encouragement during difficult times.

Together, we can conquer any challenge that comes our way.

Building a strong support system of allies and advocates is crucial for overcoming challenges, bouncing back from setbacks, and emerging even stronger and more resilient in the face of adversity. In summary, developing resilience is absolutely essential for conquering the inevitable obstacles and hurdles in life and business. By fostering a positive outlook, prioritizing self-care, seeking assistance from others, and reframing challenges as opportunities for growth, you can cultivate the resilience necessary to overcome hardships, adapt to change, and emerge as a stronger, more resilient individual. Embracing a resilient mindset will not only help you thrive in the face of adversity, but also lead you to achieve greater success and fulfillment in all aspects of your life. resilient mindset will undoubtedly empower you to not just survive, but thrive in the face of adversity, enabling you to achieve greater success and fulfillment in every aspect of your life.

Last chapter 9. Navigating Change:

Adapting and Thriving in a Dynamic WorldIn today's fast-paced and constantly changing world, mastering the skill of navigating change is crucial for achieving personal and professional success. Adapting to new technologies, market trends, and life events is a must in order to excel in a dynamic environment. To ensure you come out on top, there are several key strategies you can employ. First and foremost, maintaining a positive mindset and viewing change as an opportunity for growth and learning is essential. Embrace change as a chance to challenge yourself and expand your capabilities, rather than resisting it. Additionally, being flexible and open-minded is key to navigating change successfully. This means being willing to try new approaches, take on new responsibilities, and step out of your comfort zone.

By staying adaptable and eager to learn, you can stay ahead of the curve and thrive in a rapidly changing world. Effective communication is also vital in navigating change.

Read my book: on How to Navigate Business and Create Wealth

Keeping open lines of communication with colleagues, friends, and family members can help you stay informed about changes happening around you and gather support when needed. Articulating your needs and concerns can also help you navigate change more smoothly. Lastly, prioritizing self-care during times of change is crucial. Engaging in self-care activities like exercise, meditation, and spending time with loved ones can help you stay resilient and adapt more effectively.

By following these strategies and approaching change with a positive mindset, flexibility, communication, and self-care, you can successfully navigate change and thrive in a dynamic world.

I am truly grateful to all those who have dedicated their time to reading this short book from cover to end. I sincerely believe that you will discover immense value in its contents, just as much as I have in compiling it. This book serves as a testament to the trials and triumphs our business has endured.

My reputation is built on a relentless commitment to driving your business success through absolute honesty and integrity. I intentionally partner with those who are truly eager for guidance, striving for growth and innovation, or seeking impactful solutions to their challenges. Together, we can unlock your full potential and achieve remarkable results.

My ultimate wish is that you create wealth, and lead a life filled with happiness and joy, confidently achieving your own goals and success.

www.ingramcontent.com/pod-product-compliance
Lightning Source LLC
Chambersburg PA
CBHW070348230526
45471CB00006B/2471